John Thompson's
MELODY ALL THE WAY

A SERIES OF SUPPLEMENTARY PIANO BOOKS DESIGNED TO BE USED WITH

THE MODERN COURSE FOR THE PIANO

BOOK 1-b

•

BASED EXCLUSIVELY
ON
WELL KNOWN AIRS

THE WILLIS MUSIC COMPANY

CONTENTS

FOREWORD

The MELODY ALL THE WAY series is published in response to the insistent pleas of countless piano teachers who fully subscribe to the author's standards of teaching material and teaching ideas, but who find themselves in a quandry when two children are studying in the same family, or where neighbor children 'start' together. The heartaches that naturally arise if one child progresses somewhat faster than the other are obviated if the youngsters are not using the same book.

The MELODY ALL THE WAY series is therefore planned, not in any sense to *supplant* the MODERN COURSE FOR THE PIANO, but is *interchangeable* with that work.

Some teachers find it sound practice to use two study books simultaneously—one, of course, serving the purpose of a supplementary book for sight-reading and additional practice material.

Book 1-b of the MELODY ALL THE WAY series would be ideal for this use in connection with the *second half* of "The First Grade Book" from THE MODERN COURSE FOR THE PIANO.

Each course however, is complete in itself and may be *used singly* to lay a complete and correct musical foundation.

FAMILIAR AIRS

In so far as possible, the musical examples in MELODY ALL THE WAY have been adapted from familiar airs—folk tunes, themes from symphonies, well-known piano solos, songs, etc. This has an advantage for the young student: getting away from cut-and-dried text, and giving him the thrill of performing, in simplified version, music which he hears frequently on the radio, phonograph records, etc.

PLAYING WITH EXPRESSION

There is no sound reason why the elementary pianist should not be required to play with *musical expression* and *understanding*. The simplest melody can be interesting if played with definite intention. Real interpretation consists of more than simply following the marks of dynamics. It includes *color*—the result of employing various Touches.

Even a beginner can master the Touches. Taught in their fundamental form, they offer no real proble n, and the result in stimulating real musicianship will richly reward the efforts of teacher and pupil alike.

THE HANON STUDIES –FOR DEVELOPING THE TOUCHES

John Thompson's edition of the Hanon Studies presents exercises carefully designed to develop these fundamental touches. The studies are arranged in Quarter Notes, and each page is attractively illustrated and titled.

The Phrasing Touch, Finger Legato, Finger Staccato, Wrist Staccato, Forearm Staccato and Legato, Portamento, Rotary Motion, etc., are treated in consecutive order.

To accomplish *maximum* results, these Hanon Studies should be assigned early in Book 1-a and continued throughout the progress of Book 1-b. The improvement in interpretation will be readily apparent.

TEMPO

While each example bears a Tempo indication—*Moderato, Andante, Allegro,* etc., the *actual* rate of speed should be decided by the teacher, since·pupils vary so widely in ability. While encouraging an increased tempo in review work, the wise teacher never allows speed to go beyond the point of *precision*—always a most important objective.

FIRST GRADE ETUDES

For *general* technical work the author's FIRST GRADE ETUDES are especially designed for pupils in this grade. They may be assigned, at the discretion of the teacher, either *toward the end* of Book 1-a or *at the beginning* of Book 1-b.

The author has kept in mind the fact that all examples, even technical exercises, must be tuneful if the young pupil's interest is to be retained.

Properly used, the FIRST GRADE ETUDES becomes at once a means of developing *independence, strength, evenness* and *speed* of finger action, together with *reading* and *expression*.

CHRISTMAS CAROLS

At the back of this book, page 40, two Christmas Carols are presented.

Since pupils vary in progress and begin piano study at different times of the year, it was obviously impossible to place the Carols in the exact spot in the book that would coincide with the Christmas season.

No matter what part of the book the pupil is studying, these Carols should be assigned as supplementary solos in time to be learned for the Christmas Recital Program.

THE STUDENTS SERIES
(Teaching pieces in sheet form)

Supplementary solos form an important part of teaching material. A "new piece" is always a visible sign of progress to the pupil.

In this busy age, where practice hours are apt to be "streamlined" in keeping with everything else, the teaching pieces must have definite pianistic or musical value.

A carefully chosen composition will offer not only enjoyment to the pupil, but will at the same time, be of educational value—thus speeding progress since every moment at the keyboard *counts*.

John Thompson's STUDENTS SERIES comprise compositions from various composers, each selected on its merits. A list of such compositions, suitable for use with this book is shown on page 43.

MUSIC WRITING BOOKS
(For home work)

Every worth-while teacher knows the value of Music Writing Books for home work.

The author has designed three such Writing Books for the elementary pianist. The time of their assignment is a matter of individual preference on the part of the teacher but they should be used in the following order; THE NOTE SPELLER, THE SCALE SPELLER and THE CHORD SPELLER.

CERTIFICATE OF MERIT

A Certificate of Merit has been included on page 45 as recognition of the successful completion of this book. It should be signed and dated by the teacher.

J. T.

THUMB UNDER

From
WALTZ

Allegretto

Johann Strauss

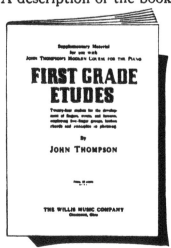

Teacher's Note

At this point the pupil should be assigned John Thompson's FIRST GRADE ETUDES. A description of the book is shown below.

This book is intended to lay a foundation in technique for the FIRST GRADE piano student. The author has kept in mind the fact that all examples, even technical exercises, must be tuneful if the young pupil's interest is to be retained.

Only elementary pianistic figures have been employed, built for the most part on five-finger groups (the forerunner of the scale) and broken triads (preparation for extended arpeggios to follow later on). Properly used, the book becomes at once a means of developing *Independence*, *Strength* and *Evenness of Finger Action*, together with *Reading and Expression*.

Examples in *Phrasing*, *Wrist Staccato* and the use of the *Forearm* have been included.

THUMB UNDER
Preparatory Studies

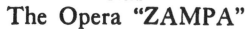

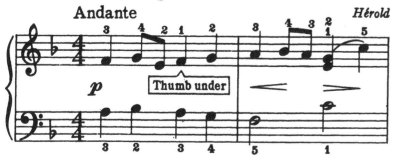

Zampa was a pirate in the Opera of that name.

Camille, the heroine of the opera, is alarmed for her father's safety as he sets out to meet his incoming fleet of ships, threatened by the pirates.

She sings the air shown here as she prays for his safe return. **From**

The Opera "ZAMPA"

Andante   *Hérold*

NEW KEY— D MAJOR

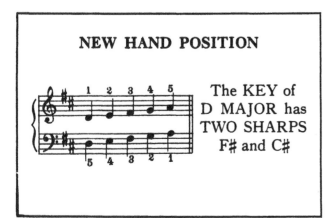

NEW HAND POSITION

The KEY of
D MAJOR has
TWO SHARPS
F♯ and C♯

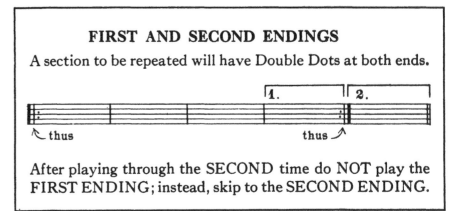

FIRST AND SECOND ENDINGS

A section to be repeated will have Double Dots at both ends.

thus 　　　　　　　　　　　thus

After playing through the SECOND time do NOT play the
FIRST ENDING; instead, skip to the SECOND ENDING.

From

THE MILL

Adolf Jensen

Allegro moderato

Play the Scale and Broken Chord of D Major.

W. M. Co. 6603

A NTON RUBINSTEIN was born in Russia and when he was five showed great talent. When he was eleven the great Liszt proclaimed him a genius.

One of the most popular compositions he ever wrote was the "Melody in F", which is still a favorite over the radio and with piano students everywhere.

From

MELODY in F

Anton Rubinstein

Hand Position

Additional Bass Notes for the Left Hand

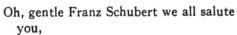

NEW KEY—A MAJOR

The KEY of A MAJOR has THREE SHARPS—
F#, C# and G#

Practice the Left Hand alone first as a Preparatory Study.

Oh, gentle Franz Schubert we all salute you,
Beautiful Music we sing to-day.
Comes echo'ing clear from happier ages
When Old Vienna was young and gay.

From

WALTZ

Franz Schubert

Moderato M.M. 80-160

Change fingering

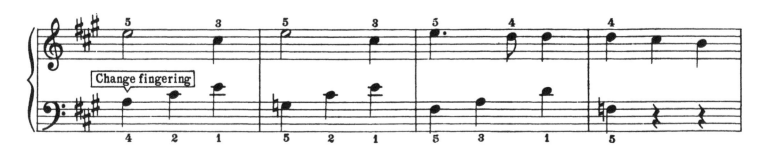

Play the Scale and Broken Chord of A Major

From
FUNERAL MARCH

Very slowly and solemnly

Frédéric Chopin

Suggestion for supplementary solo in sheet form.

PROCESSION OF THE SEVEN DWARFS by Lois Long is a fine follow-up piece with both hands in the Bass Clef.   See page 43.

W.M.Co.6602

TWO-NOTE PHRASES IN SKIPS

Recital Piece

From

HUMORESQUE

Anton Dvořák

LUDWIG VAN BEETHOVEN was born in Bonn, a city on the Rhine river. He began to study music when he was four years old, and when he was eight he played violin very well. Beethoven is acknowledged the greatest instrumental composer the world has produced. He had a very busy and full life; much joy and many sorrows. His magnificent music is played by all the great orchestras to this day. Listen when next a Beethoven Symphony is scheduled to be played on the radio. He left the world much richer for having lived in it.

LUDWIG VAN BEETHOVEN
1770-1827

From
RONDINO

Ludwig van Beethoven

D.S. (*Dal Segno*) *al fine* means go back to sign (𝄋) and play to *Fine*

STACCATO NOVELTY

From
THE MUSIC BOX

Anatol Liadow

Allegretto

Right Hand sustained

Play both hands TWO octaves higher than written

Left Hand with sharp staccato

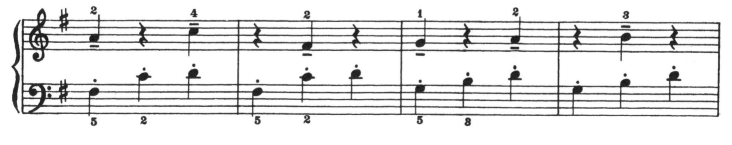

l.h.over

To produce the effect of a Music Box press the damper pedal down *half way* and hold it throughout.
Release it sharply on the last staccato note of the piece.
Play the left hand with brittle staccato.
The right hand notes marked thus, $\bar{\rho}$ are to be played *sostenuto*—in a sustained manner.

W.M.Co.6603

THE DOTTED-EIGHTH NOTE

MARCH OF THE TOREADORS

From
The Opera "CARMEN"

Georges Bizet

In March Tempo

B Flat Major has
TWO FLATS
B♭ and E♭

BRIDAL CHORUS
From
The Opera "LOHENGRIN"

Richard Wagner

Slow March Time

NEW KEY—E♭ MAJOR

E Flat Major has
THREE FLATS
B♭, E♭ and A♭

WINGS

Up above the houses glides the soaring plane

Cutting through the clouds and back to sun again

You can be the captain of a ship at sea

Just to fly a plane would be the life for me!

MELODY IN THE LEFT HAND
Right Hand Staccato Thirds

FRANZ SCHUBERT is known as the greatest song writer that ever lived. He was born in Austria near Vienna and when he was ten years old he was singing in a church choir, and had already composed some little songs and piano pieces.

The music of Schubert comes into our homes constantly over the radio. This master lived only 31 years and yet he wrote more than 1,100 compositions; and of these nearly 600 are songs.

From
THE UNFINISHED SYMPHONY

Andante moderato

Franz Schubert

W. M. Co. 6603

From

JUST A SONG AT TWILIGHT

J. L. Molloy

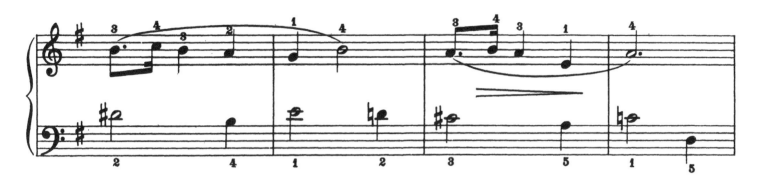

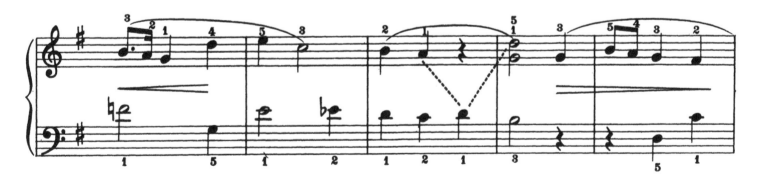

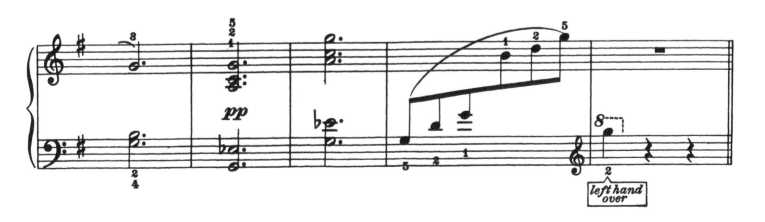

NEW KEY—E MAJOR

1st Position   **2nd Position**

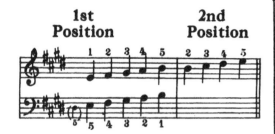

The KEY of E MAJOR has FOUR SHARPS—F#, C#, G# and D#.

FELIX MENDELSSOHN was born in Hamburg, Germany of wealthy and musical parents.

At eleven years of age he was already seriously interested in composition. He loved fairy stories and much of his music reflects this liking.

He wrote many beautiful piano pieces and the "Rondo Capriccioso" is one of the most famous.

From

"RONDO CAPRICCIOSO"

Felix Mendelssohn

G IUSEPPE VERDI was born to a poor inn-keeper and his wife who lived at the foot of the Apennine Mountains.

In his time Italy was ruled by a foreign nation and as Verdi's operas all breathed patriotism, he was the idol of his country.

The little composition which you are now to study, is one of the most popular and lasting airs ever written. You will have heard it many times on your radio.

LA DONNA E MOBILE
from the Opera "RIGOLETTO"

Giuseppe Verdi

Teacher's Note: See page 43 for list of supplementary solos in sheet form.

W.M.Co.6603

NEW KEY—A♭ MAJOR

Hand Position

The KEY of A♭ MAJOR has FOUR FLATS—
B♭, E♭ A♭ and D♭

Play the followong piece with your best singing tone.

Lily, lily, white and gold,
Gleaming from the water cold,
You shall reign like any queen
'Til the Autumn winds grow keen.

DAY DREAMS

Andante moderato

Preparatory Exercise

From

HUNGARIAN RHAPSODIE

No. 12

Franz Liszt

From "ROSAMUNDE"

Franz Schubert

Allegro animato

mp

Fine

mp

D. S. al Fine

Recital Material

For costume recitals, John Thompson's COVERED WAGON SUITE will be found ideal. It is descriptive of the days of '49 and all five numbers lie comfortably under the hands.

W.M.Co. 6603

FREDERIC CHOPIN
1810 - 1849

When Frédéric Chopin was a little boy, the Polish people called him a second Mozart, and we know that he played a concerto in public before he was nine years old. He was very imaginative and sensitive to beauty, and one great Polish actor expressed the opinion that he would have done well on the stage. He wrote a great deal of beautiful music during his short life-time, including nineteen Nocturnes.

The word Nocturne means night song. The following is an adaptation of one of his best-loved 'night songs'.

From

NOCTURNE

Frédéric Chopin

Liszt at the age of 14
Courtesy "The Musical Quarterly"

FRANZ LISZT was born in a little town in Hungary. He was a child-wonder—playing a public concert at the age of nine. Many of his compositions are inspired by Hungarian Gipsy themes.

He was a most brilliant pianist and a beloved teacher, helping and inspiring many pupils who became concert artists.

Born 1811 — Died 1886

From

HUNGARIAN RHAPSODIE
No. 2

Franz Liszt

From
MARCHE MILITAIRE

Franz Schubert

In brisk March Tempo

Note Change of Key

Watch the fingering as the hands change position

W.M.Co.6603

CHORD PLAYING

At Prince Radziwill's in 1829

Among the many beautiful and immortal works of Chopin are the Twenty-Four Preludes—one in each major and minor key.

The Prelude on this page is an adaptation of one of the most popular of these beloved piano compositions.

From

PRELUDE IN C MINOR

Frédéric Chopin

Be very careful of the fingering

Andante

Be sure to practice each hand separately until you have mastered the fingering.

W.M.Co.6603

SIXTEENTH NOTES
From
UNDER THE LEAVES

Thoma

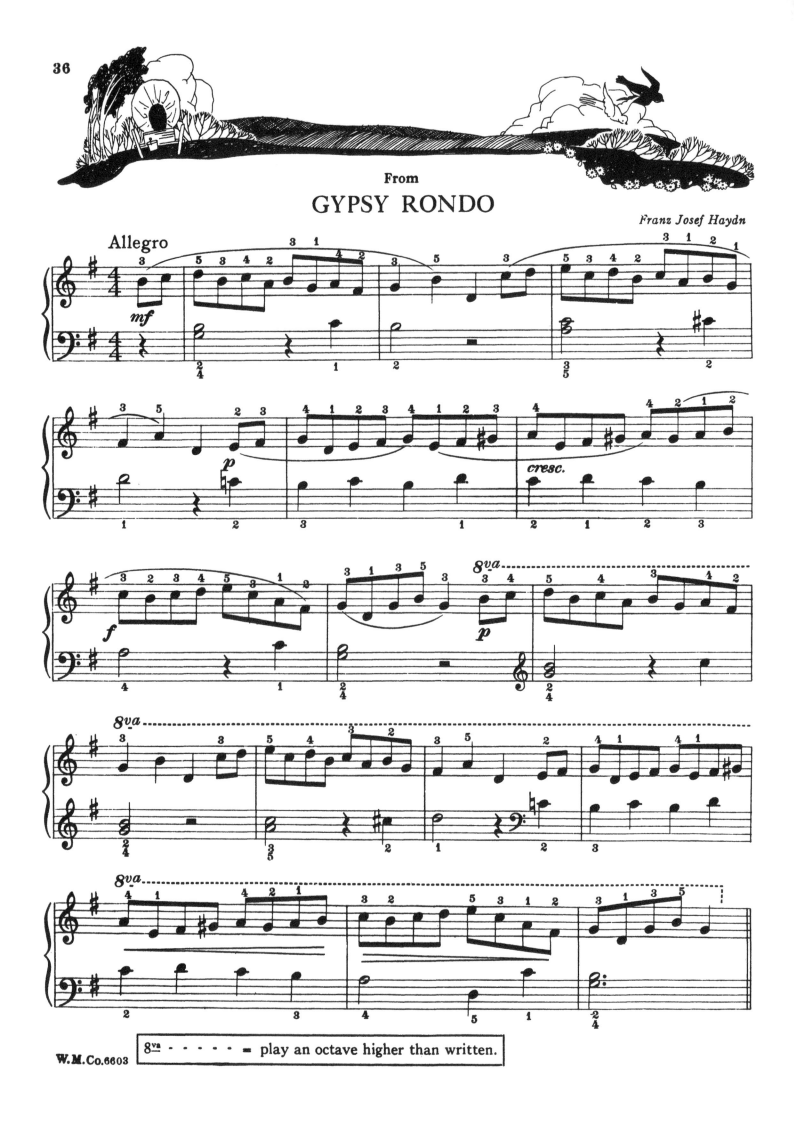

From

GYPSY RONDO

Franz Josef Haydn

8va - - - - - - = play an octave higher than written.

From

VALSE, Op. 34, No 2

Frédéric Chopin

JOHN PHILIP SOUSA was born in Washington, D. C. He was an eminent band-master and probably the most popular composer of band marches the world has produced. He was known as "The March King". When he was eight years old he was playing violin in a dancing school and at the age of sixteen, conducted a theatre orchestra. His best known marches are "The Stars and Stripes Forever", "High School Cadets" and "The Washington Post March".

From
THE WASHINGTON POST MARCH

John Philip Sousa

JOLLY OLD SAINT NICHOLAS

Traditional

2. When the clock is striking twelve,
   When I'm fast asleep,
Down the chimney broad and black,
   With your pack you'll creep;
All the stockings you will find
   Hanging in a row;
Mine will be the shortest one,
   You'll be sure to know.

3. Johnny wants a pair of skates;
   Susy wants a sled;
Nellie wants a picture book;
   Yellow, blue and red;
Now I think I'll leave to you
   What to give the rest;
Choose for me, dear Santa Claus,
   You will know the best.

GOD REST YOU MERRY, GENTLEMEN

Old English

2. From God, our heav'nly Father,
   A blessed angel came;
   And unto certain shepherds
   Brought tidings of the same;
   How that in Bethlehem was born
   The Son of God by name.
   Refrain.

3. The shepherds at those tidings,
   Rejoiced much in mind,
   And left their flocks a-feeding,
   In tempest, storm, and wind;
   And went to Bethlehem straightway,
   The Son of God to find.
   Refrain.

W.M.Co.6603

GLOSSARY OF TERMS, SIGNS
AND ABBREVIATIONS USED IN THIS BOOK

Signs or Abbreviations	Terms	Meaning
>	accent	To emphasize or stress a certain note or beat
	allegretto	Light and lively
	allegro	Fast
	andante	Slow
	andantino	Slow—but not as slow as *andante*
	animato	With animation
	arpeggio	In the style of a harp—broken chord
	a tempo	Resume original tempo
	crescendo	A gradual increase in the tone
D.C.	Da Capo	Return to beginning
D.C. al Fine	Da Capo al Fine	Return to beginning and play to *Fine*
	diminuendo	A gradual decrease in the tone
	espressivo	Expressively
Fine	Finale	The end
f	forte	Loud
ff	fortissimo	Very loud
	largo	Very slowly
	legato	Connected, bound together
mf	mezzo forte	Moderately loud
mp	mezzo piano	Moderately soft
	moderato	At a moderate tempo
	molto	Much
	Nocturne	Night Song
8va or 8	octave above	Play all notes under this sign one octave higher than written
⌢⊙	pause	To hold or pause, according to taste
p	piano	Softly
pp	pianissimo	Very softly
	poco	Little
rit.	ritard	A gradual slowing of the tempo
	sostenuto	Sustained—with singing quality
	staccato	Detached
	tempo	Time—rate of speed

Some interesting facts about
JOHN THOMPSON

HONORS CONFERRED

DOCTOR OF MUSIC DEGREE awarded for distinguished work in furthering Musical Education by means of his Piano Teaching Material.
FELLOW OF NATIONAL COLLEGE—Toronto, Canada.

TEACHER

DIRECTOR EMERITUS—Conservatory of Music, Kansas City, Mo.
Former DIRECTOR PIANO DEPARTMENT—Indianapolis Conservatory of Music.
Former VICE-PRESIDENT—Leefson-Hille Conservatory, Philadelphia, Penna.

CONCERT PIANIST

John Thompson has made two European Concert Tours and numerous American tours and has appeared as soloist with the following well-known orchestras:

London Symphony	Philadelphia Orchestra
Boston Symphony	Verdi Italian Symphony
St. Louis Symphony	Kansas City Symphony

COMPOSER

John Thompson's teaching material, in addition to its unrivalled popularity in the United States, is widely used in CANADA, the BRITISH ISLES, AUSTRALIA, NEW ZEALAND, countries in CENTRAL and SOUTH AMERICA and in far away CHINA. Special editions for some of these foreign countries have been printed. A number of his books have been transcribed and printed in Braille for the use of the blind.

JOHN THOMPSON'S STUDENTS SERIES

A carefully selected list of Teaching Pieces, suitable for use with Books 1-a and 1-b

of

"MELODY ALL THE WAY"

Title	Composer	Key
BARNYARD FROLICS	Vivian Blackford	G

Melody and phrasing in the right hand; broken chord accompaniment in the left.

BOGEY MAN, THE......Lois Long............Am
Humoresque, with special emphasis on staccato, sudden accents and phrasing.

COBBLER, COBBLER....Louise Christine Rebe.G
Descriptive, showing tapping of cobbler's hammer. Contrast between staccato and legato.

DUTCH TWINS, THE......Willa Ward.........C
Humorous Dutch dance depicting dialogue between Gretchen and Hans. Develops tonal contrast and two-note phrasing.

FOREST DAWN.........John Thompson......C
Employs broken chords and trills, describing sunrise and bird-calls.

HOE CAKE SHUFFLE...Charles Leslie........G
Little study in syncopation. Southern style.

IN THE SWING.........June Waldo..........C
Melody playing in the right hand, making use of extended phrases.

LE TAMBORIN.........Rameau-Thompson...Cm
Famous old classic specially adapted for the First Grader. Contrast between staccato and legato.

LITTLE ROCKING HORSE, THE
                    J. J. Ames............C
*A delightful melody, simple but most effective.
The left hand is required to play two-note and three-note phrases in accompaniment.*

MARCH OF THE SPOOKS
                    Edmund Haines......Cm
Staccato in both hands. Appropriate Hallow'een tune.

MARCHE SLAV....Tschaikowsky-Thompson...Am
This famous melody is arranged for the right hand against a simple accompaniment in the left.

MOCCASIN DANCE......Lois Long............Am
Descriptive novelty developing melody playing and phrasing.

ON THE LEVEE.........June Waldo..........C
Syncopated tune in the style of a Negro Spiritual.

PROCESSION OF THE SEVEN DWARFS
                    Lois Long............G
An attractive number in which both hands play in Bass Clef. Stresses staccato and accents.

SWAYING SILVER BIRCHES
                    Charles Leslie........C
Melody in the left hand. Broken chord accompaniment phrased in twos, in the right hand.

TWILIGHT LULLABY...Edmund Haines......C
Beautiful but simple melody in the right hand with a slight modern "flavor".

COVERED WAGON SUITE
                    John Thompson
Miniture suite of five First Grade pieces descriptive of important episodes in the days of 1849. Excellent material for pupils' recitals. Handsomely illustrated.

TWO PIANOS — FOUR HANDS

TOY SHIPS.............Mortimer Manning...C
A charming recital number. Both parts lie well within First Grade.

SUPPLEMENTARY BOOKS

Suitable for use with this book

A First Grade edition—in quarter notes—of this standard work for the piano.

It has been specially designed to develop **fundamental touches** in piano playing. Phrasing, finger legato, finger staccato, wrist staccato, f o r e a r m s t a c c a t o, portamento playing, rotary motion etc.—all treated in consecutive order with illustrations, titles and complete explanatory text.

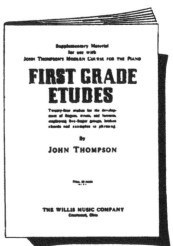

This book is intended to lay a foundation in technique for the **First Grade** piano student. The author has kept in mind the fact that all examples, even technical exercises, must be tuneful if the young pupil's interest is to be retained. Properly used, the b o o k becomes at once a means of developing **Independence**; **Strength** and **Evenness of finger Action**; together with **Reading and Expression**.

FOR BOYS

LET'S JOIN THE ARMY

This book has been especially dedicated to the **American Boy.**

During instruction, the teacher assumes the role of **Commanding Officer**, giving directions in "order" or "commands" similar to the military manner Exercises are presented in the form of pieces to develop **finger legato, w r i s t staccato, arm staccato and phrasing attack.** Many examples, built upon bugle calls have been introduced to stress rhythm, a musical characteristic of most boys.

FOR GIRLS

FOR GIRLS WHO PLAY

Good educational music is so universally in vogue among piano teachers that it is quite "the fashion" nowadays to play only good music.

In this book, designed especially for girl pupils, there are 31 pieces progressing g r a d u a l l y in technical sequence, each piece written with a definite purpose.

Subjects to interest every girl have been masterfully presented in music and verse.

Certificate of Merit

This certifies that

....

has successfully completed

BOOK 1-b

OF

JOHN THOMPSON'S
"MELODY ALL THE WAY"

and is eligible for promotion to

BOOK 2-a

Teacher

Date...